Amazing Airplanes

Activity Book

Tony Mitton • Ant Parker

KINGFISHER

NEW YORK

KINGFISHER
LONDON & NEW YORK

Text copyright © Tony Mitton 2002, 2016
Illustrations copyright © Ant Parker 2002, 2016

Published in the United States by Kingfisher,
175 Fifth Ave., New York, NY 10010
Kingfisher is an imprint of Macmillan Children's Books, London

Series editor: Catherine Ard
Series design: Anthony Hannant (LittleRedAnt)

Distributed in the U.S. and Canada by Macmillan,
175 Fifth Ave., New York, NY 10010

Kingfisher books are available for special promotions and premiums.
For details contact: Special Markets Department, Macmillan, 175 Fifth Ave.,
New York, NY 10010.
For more information, please visit www.kingfisherbooks.com

Library of Congress Cataloging-in-Publication data
has been applied for.

ISBN 978-0-7534-7255-2

Printed in China

9 8 7 6 5 4 3 2 1

1TR/0116/LFG/UG/120WF

My passport

Name ....

Age ....   Draw yourself here. ↪

Let's go on an airplane!

Don't forget to:

☐ Pack your suitcase   ☐ Check in at the airport

☐ Load your baggage   ☐ Meet the crew

☐ Find your seat   ☐ Enjoy your flight

Pack!

It's time to go on vacation! Pack everything you need.

Look at the list and tick the box for each thing you see in the picture below.

Which thing is missing from the picture? Put a cross beside it.

Go!

The airport is the place to go to take a trip by plane.

Draw a line to show Freddy Rabbit the way to the airport.

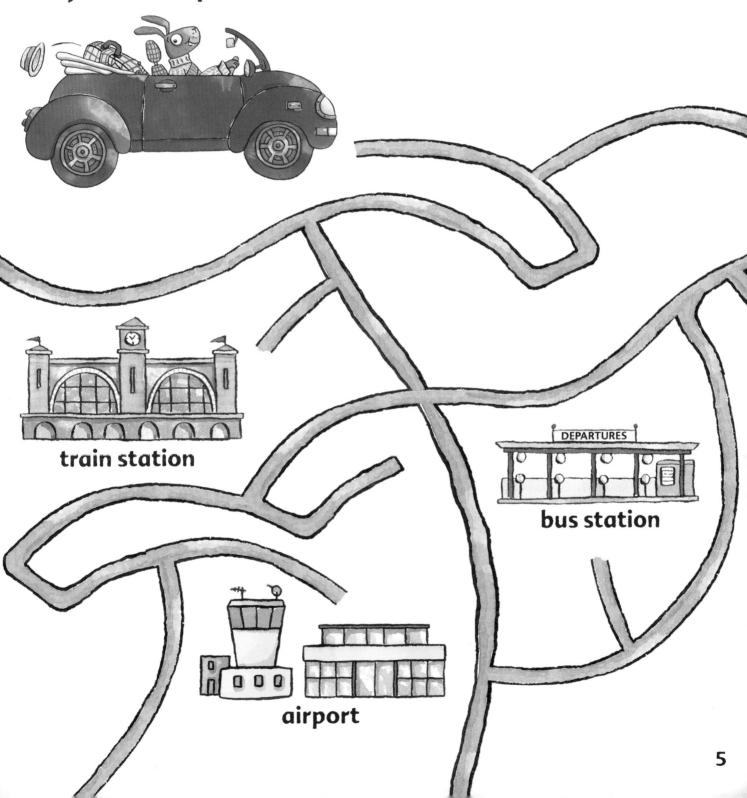

train station

DEPARTURES

bus station

airport

Tickets!

It's time to check in at the terminal. You will need to show your ticket.

Draw lines to join each passenger with the right suitcase. The first one has been done for you.

Danny Dog   Sally Bird   Ollie Mouse   Freddy Rabbit

1 — F.R.

2 — O.M.

3 — S.B.

4 — D.D.

Sally Bird has lost her ticket! Can you find it on this page?

Heave!

Baggage of all shapes and sizes goes on a conveyor belt to the plane.

Put the baggage in order by writing a number under each case. Make the smallest case number 1 and the biggest number 4.

Color in the suitcases to finish the pattern.

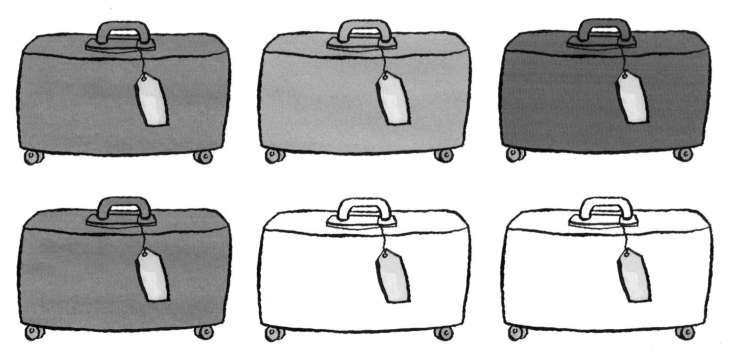

Watch!

See the planes take off and land while you wait for your flight.

How many planes of each color can you count? Write the numbers in the boxes.

☐ green   ☐ yellow   ☐ orange   ☐ red

Hurry!

Take the walkway to the plane as soon as you are told.

Help this passenger find the route to gate 7. You have to pass each gate from 1 to 6 on the way.

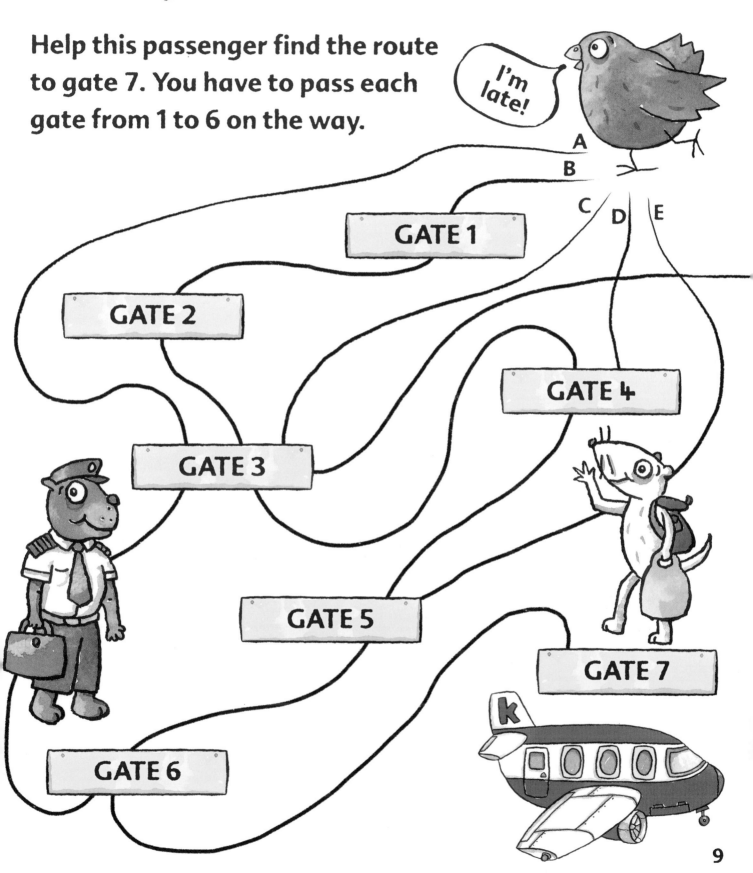

I'm late!

A
B
C
D
E

GATE 1

GATE 2

GATE 4

GATE 3

GATE 5

GATE 7

GATE 6

k

Load!

The ground crew load the baggage into the plane's hold.

How many of each thing can you count in the big picture? Write your answers in the boxes.

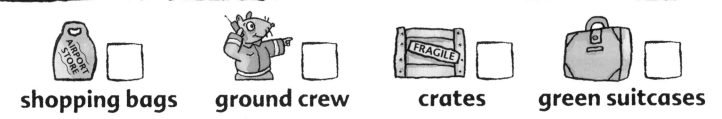

shopping bags   ground crew   crates   green suitcases

Can you spot Ollie Mouse's paper airplane in the scene above?

10

Fill!

The plane is filled with fuel to make its engines work during the flight.

Which fuel tanker is filling the plane?
Follow the pipes and color in the correct tanker.

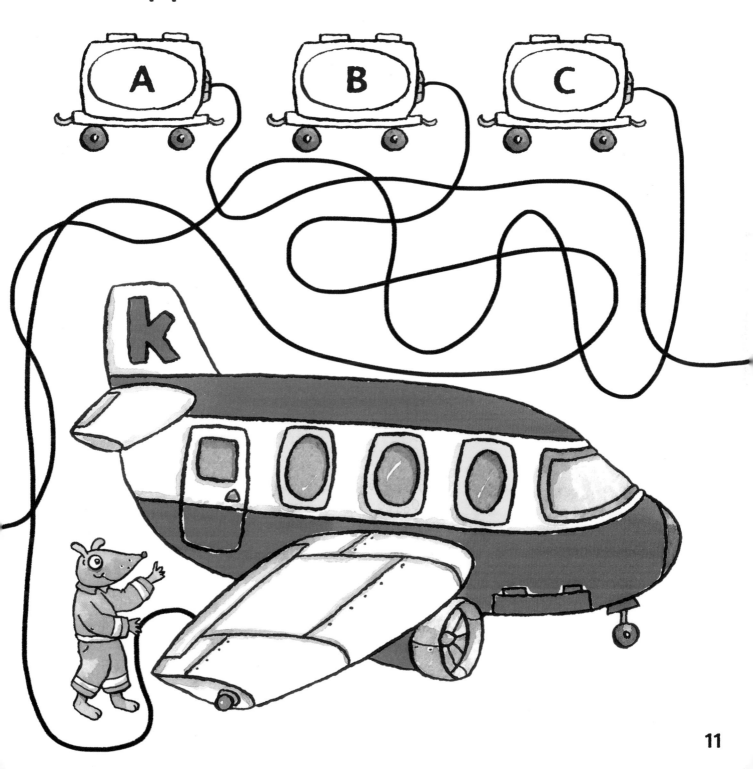

Airplane!

Each part of the airplane does a different job.

Can you find all these parts on the plane?

Finish writing the labels. One has already been done for you.

nose
The rounded part at the front of the plane.

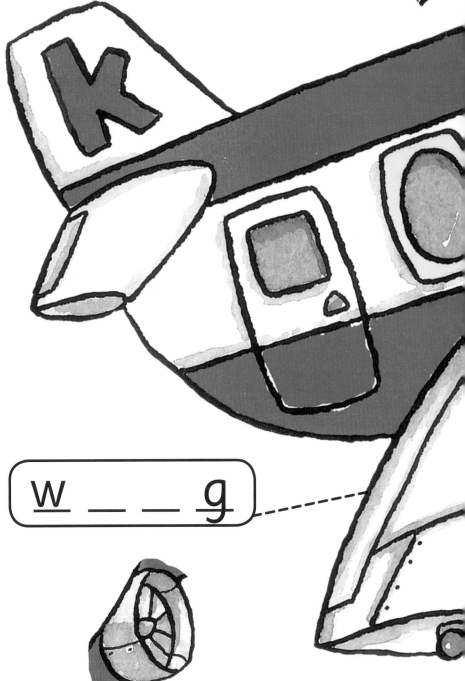

w _ _ g

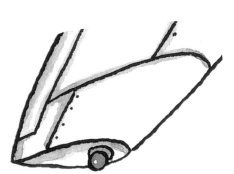

wing
The wings are hollow to make them light. They are smooth so they move through the air easily.

jet engine
The engines blow out air and gas to push the plane forward. The gas is made by burning fuel.

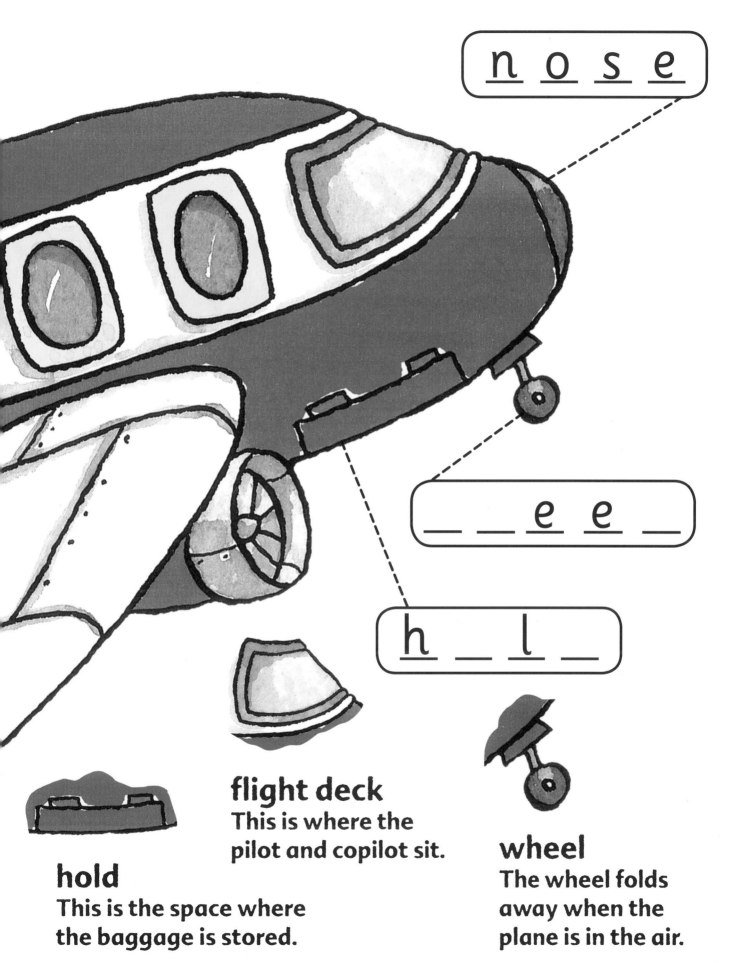

n o s e

_ _ _ e e _

h _ l _

flight deck
This is where the
pilot and copilot sit.

hold
This is the space where
the baggage is stored.

wheel
The wheel folds
away when the
plane is in the air.

Meet!

The flight crew prepare the airplane and welcome you on board.

Finish coloring in the crew's uniforms.
Use pens that match the colored dots.

The flight attendant looks after the passengers.

The pilot flies the plane.

Sit!

Each seat has a letter and a number to help you find your place.

Look at the letter and number each passenger is thinking of. Draw a line to lead each person to the seat with the matching letter and number.

Wait!

It's busy at the airport! Before it reaches the runway each plane must wait in a line.

Draw lines to match each pair of planes.
Which plane doesn't have a matching one?

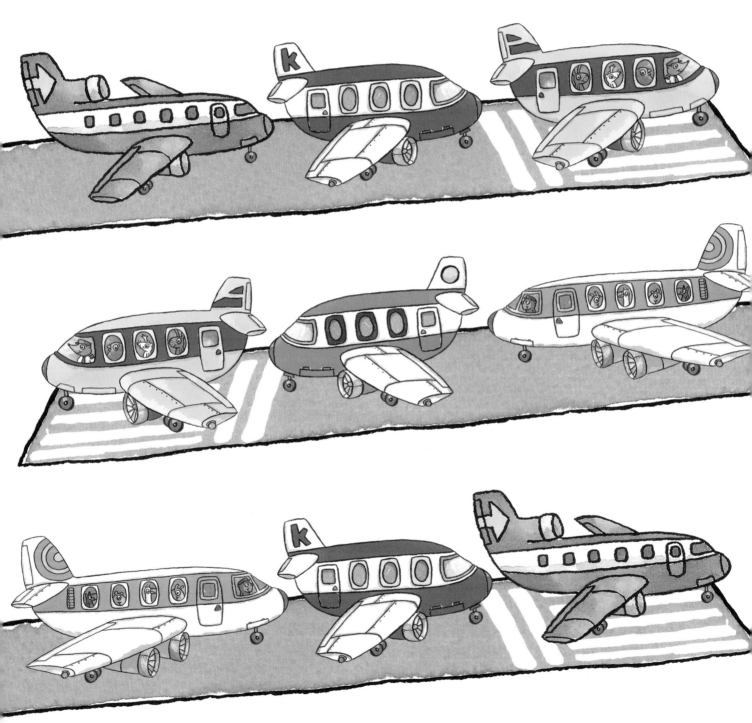

Ready!

The pilot radios the control tower to check the runway is clear.

Spot five differences between these two pictures.
Circle each difference you find in the bottom picture.

Zoom!

The plane zooms along the runway and soars into the sky.

Color in this airplane to match the one above.

Which two passengers have swapped seats?

Look!

Look out of the window and see the land below.

Which square completes the view from the window?
Draw a circle around the correct one.

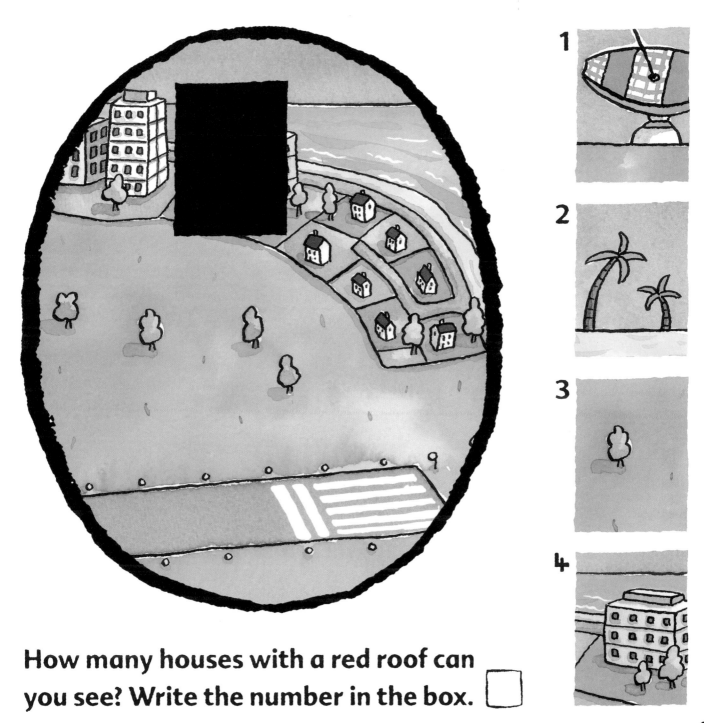

1

2

3

4

How many houses with a red roof can you see? Write the number in the box. ☐

Relax!

Once the plane is in the air you can relax and enjoy the flight.

Find the passenger who is...

 sleeping

 reading

 watching TV

 drinking

Spot these things in the picture and color them to match.

Yum!

The flight attendant brings trays of tasty food to eat.

Menu

fish

peas

fries

apple

Which two things are missing from this food tray? Check the menu and draw them in.

Bump!

When the journey's over, the pilot lands the plane.

Find the shadow below that matches the airplane. Write the correct letter in the box. ☐

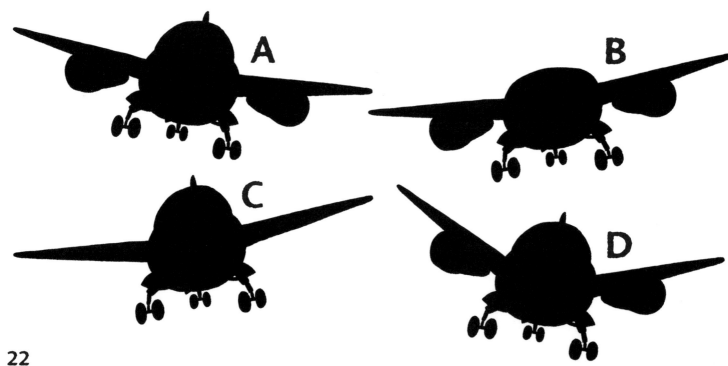

Hurrah!

Give a cheer—you're finally here. You've flown a long, long way.

Put the pictures of Freddy Rabbit's trip in order from 1 to 4. Write the numbers in the boxes.

Put these numbers in the correct order, starting with the smallest number: 5 3 1 4 7 6

Answers

Page 4
The camera is missing.

Page 5

Page 6
Sally Bird—3, Ollie Mouse—2, Freddy Rabbit—1.
The lost ticket is in front of Danny Dog's suitcase.

Page 7
Blue case—1, green case—2, orange case—3, purple case—4.

Page 8
1 green, 3 yellow, 2 orange, 4 red.

Page 9
Route B passes all the gates.

Page 10
1 shopping bag, 3 ground crew, 2 crates, 2 green suitcases.
Ollie Mouse's paper airplane is by the big, red airplane.

Page 11
Fuel tanker B.

Pages 12—13
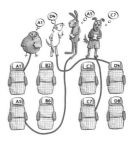

Page 15

Page 16
The blue airplane doesn't have a matching one.

Page 17

Page 18
Sally Bird and Freddy Rabbit have swapped seats.

Page 19
Square 4 completes the view.
There are 7 houses with a red roof.

Page 20
Cat is sleeping, Bird is reading, Freddy Rabbit is watching TV, Danny Dog is drinking.

Page 21
The fish and the apple are missing from the tray.

Page 22
Shadow A matches the airplane.

Page 23
A = 4, B = 3, C = 2, D = 1.
The correct order is: 1 3 4 5 6 7.